Whiteboard and WanderLust

The Seeds of Wanderlust

Sharri Holroyd

Whiteboard and WanderLust

Copyright © *Sharri Holroyd,* 2025

All Rights Reserved

This book is subject to the condition that no part of this book is to be reproduced, transmitted in any form or means; electronic or mechanical, stored in a retrieval system, photocopied, recorded, scanned, or otherwise. Any of these actions require the proper written permission of the author.

Contents

Chapter 1 "Fine Isn't Enough" 4

Chapter 2 Ctrl Alt Escape 9

Chapter 3 A Keyring, a One-Way Ticket, and Everything I Didn't Say 13

Chapter 4 Touchdown in Chaos 19

Chapter 5 Ban Phe Bootcamp 23

Chapter 6 Lessons & Laughter 27

Chapter 7 Magic, Mangoes & Moonlit Misadventures 30

Chapter 8 Farewells & Fittings 34

Chapter 9 Suits, Sushi & Surprise Fridges 40

Chapter 10 Behind the Beads 49

Chapter 11 Between Worlds 54

Chapter 12 Let Go, Begin Again 61

Chapter 13 Chalk Dust & Changemakers 66

Chapter 14 Letting Go, Leaping Forward 69

Chapter 1
"Fine Isn't Enough"

York was the kind of city that looked like a postcard and behaved like a quiet aunt. Polite, pretty, and just a little bit nosey if you stayed too long. The cobbled streets gleamed under a drizzle, and the Minster's towers stood like a giant sentinels frozen in prayer, their silhouette etched against the sky. The air carried the scent of roasted chestnuts from Stonegate, mingling with the faint tang of river mud from the Ouse. Tourists snapped photos of the Shambles, their laughter bouncing off the crooked walls, while locals like me ducked into alleys to avoid the chatter—and the memories.

I'd grown up in York—cobbled streets, tea rooms, drizzle. Now I lived in my own ex council house, just a few streets from where Mum still was. It was small and had an even tinier garden and wallpaper that had outlived two Prime Ministers, but I loved it—because it was mine. Mum had always been my anchor. She worked hard, smiled easily, and loved with her whole heart. We were close in the kind of way that didn't need explaining. She just knew—when I needed to talk, when I didn't, and when I just needed a cuppa and some quiet company.

I once dreamed of being a tour rep—guiding travellers through vibrant cities and hidden gems, sharing stories of culture and history under open skies. No office, just the hum of new places and faces. But York's pull was strong, and IT support paid the rent while those dreams faded into the background. Now, my days blur into a cycle of helpdesk tickets and system reboots. I stare at my monitor, fingers typing the same old fixes, and wonder when I stopped choosing my own path.

On Monday nights, I helped run a local Girl Guide group in the back hall of the local church that always smelled faintly of bleach and old coffee. I taught knots, reef, bowline, clove hitch – skills I'd never used to untie my own life and usually created chaos! I delivered pep talks about independence to ten-year-olds who were brave and loud, already more daring than I felt. I'd watch them tie their knots, small hands fumbling but determined, and think, *Maybe I'm the one who needs a lesson in letting go.*

Most of my friends were settling down—marriages, mortgages, M&S homeware sets. There were Friday nights at the same pubs, Saturday lunches and strolls round the shops. Everyone seemed fine. Comfortable, even.

And me? I was the dependable one. The tech support girl with quick fingers and a slow-burning restlessness and desperateness. At lunch, I'd peel back the clingfilm on yet another beige sandwich –ham, always ham – and stare at it, the girl at the deli counter smiling the same as yesterday. I'd nod back, same as always, and wonder when fine had become my default.

It wasn't that anything was wrong. It was that nothing was changing. I'd blink and months would pass. Same routines. Same conversations. Same beige sandwich from the corner shop.

Of course, York was a city that could charm the socks off a tourist but slowly smother a local. The cathedral bells, the scent of roasted chestnuts on Stonegate, the antique shops with windows full of forgotten silverware — it all had a storybook quality. But for those of us who'd grown up there, it could feel like being trapped inside a snow globe: lovely to look at, but always the same view.

Everyone knew everyone—or knew someone who knew someone. The kind of place where your first kiss, your driving test failures, and your choice of supermarket were common knowledge. Privacy was more of a polite illusion than a reality. I couldn't so much as buy a tin of beans without bumping into an old classmate or a neighbor who remembered the time I performed in the Brownie talent show. Smiles came easily, sure, but so did the commentary. Everyone had a version of your story, and they weren't afraid to share it over Sunday roasts or during queue chats at the Co-op.

It had been too easy to stay. I hadn't gone to university but promised myself I would in a bit, that bit stretched into years, padded out by a reliable job in IT support, midweek Zumba, and endless cups of tea poured with the quiet resignation of someone who didn't quite know what they were waiting for.

And then there was John.

We'd split up officially, yes—but "officially" can be such a slippery word. There were still the occasional texts. A casual coffee. That one late night after the pub when we ended up tangled on the sofa, laughing at a film we'd both seen a dozen times. It wasn't perfect, but it wasn't over. Not in my mind.

So, when I saw the photo—him, grinning in the Lake District, holding hands with a girl I'd never seen before, a sparkling ring on her finger and *#SaidYes* in the caption—it felt like the floor had vanished beneath me.

No warning. No conversation. Just… gone.

I didn't cry. Not at first. I went numb. Like I'd fallen asleep in one story and woken up in another, where I'd been cut from the cast without even a scene.

The whispers came quickly in York. "Did you hear about John?" "Poor Ellie, must be hard." "Well, she's always been a bit of a free spirit."

I felt like I was being written into someone else's narrative again. A footnote in someone else's happy ending. But the truth was, that ring snapped something loose in me. The ring didn't just end things with John—it ended the idea that life might quietly sort itself out if I just kept waiting. I wasn't unhappy. But I wasn't fully alive, either. I was just… fine. Fine was quiet. Fine was beige. Fine was safe.

What I needed wasn't another plus-one. I needed a way out.

Sometimes I'd take the long way home from work just to feel like I was going somewhere different. I'd watch trains leave the station and imagine where they were going. Paris. Edinburgh. Anywhere-but-here. The platforms smelled of diesel and wet concrete, and I'd stand there, boots scuffing the pavement, thinking of all the versions of me I hadn't met yet—the one who'd said yes to the tour rep job, who'd packed a bag and left the tea cooling on the counter.

That evening, I trudged home, the weight of another beige day settling into my bones and went to visit mum. She was in the kitchen, kettle humming, her hands busy with the familiar ritual of tea. She handed me a chipped mug, steam curling between us. "You're quiet tonight, love," she said, her voice soft as the drizzle outside. I shrugged, but her eyes—sharp, patient—lingered. She didn't push. She never did. Instead, she slid a biscuit across the table, the same kind she'd given me as a kid when I'd come home with scraped knees or a bruised heart.

I cradled the mug, its warmth a small anchor, and thought of the tour rep job I'd once pored over in travel magazines, the ones Mum used to leave on the coffee table "just in case." Had she seen this restlessness in me even then? "Just tired," I mumbled, but the lie felt thin under her gaze. She nodded, turning back to the kettle, but the silence between us hummed with unspoken questions—about John, about York, about the life I wasn't living.

Later that night - as many before it, I laid in bed and scrolled through travel blogs, my fingers itching to book flights I couldn't justify. My heart ached for movement—for something unplanned, unlabelled, and mine.

York had been my cradle. My comfort zone. But lately, it felt like it was tucking me in a little too tight.

And one day, without fanfare, I realised I didn't want "fine" anymore.

Chapter 2
Ctrl Alt Escape

It was 8:56 a.m. on a damp Tuesday in York, and the office smelled faintly of burnt toast and printer toner.

I sat at my desk with the familiar sinking feeling in my stomach—the one that came every weekday morning as I logged in, sipped lukewarm tea, and prepared to field yet another round of "Have you tried turning it off and on again?"

I worked on the IT support desk at Aviva, but really, who cared? It was all just acronyms and endless queues of tech issues. Headsets on, spirits off. The kind of job that slowly saps your will to live, one Outlook error message at a time.

The days blurred into each other—an endless loop of ticket numbers, Excel spreadsheets, and people who somehow still didn't know their passwords. Each problem came with a customer who was either furious, confused, or both, and my job was to keep things calm and professional. I became a master of the polite sigh and the forced smile. Inside, though, I was screaming.

It wasn't even that the job was hard. It was just that it wasn't me. I hadn't dreamed of being a headset-wearing, desk-bound cog in a corporate machine. I wanted life to feel bigger. I wanted it to *mean* something. Instead, I was spending forty hours a week explaining to grown adults how to plug in their printers. This couldn't be it. Surely?

I'd started to dread Mondays with a level of passion usually reserved for dental surgery. On particularly bad days, I'd catch myself staring at the clock, willing the hands to move faster. Minutes dragged. Hours felt like geological epochs. And that's when it hit me: I was far too young to be wishing my life away.

But I was doing it anyway. Every. Single. Day.

There were moments—odd little flashes—where I'd catch my reflection in the darkened monitor and barely recognise the girl blinking back. Twenty-something, mildly competent, thoroughly uninspired. My hair was usually tied back in a messy ponytail. I wore the same three cardigans on rotation. I ate my lunch at my desk. I was disappearing. Fading into beige.

This particularly dismal morning had started like any other—lukewarm coffee, half-hearted small talk, and an Excel sheet that had stopped calculating formulas just to spite me.

"Try refreshing the page," I half-heartedly told Derek in accounts who was surely calling for the fiftieth time. At the same time, I was already opening another tab in secret and typing into Google:

'Jobs where you can travel the world.'

It was a moment of sheer rebellion. A tiny act of defiance that felt thrillingly illegal, despite the fact that no one was watching. Except maybe Derek via screen share. But his refresh had worked and he'd just discovered the "filter by color" function in Excel, so he was otherwise occupied.

That's when I found it. TEFL. Teaching English as a Foreign Language.

I'd never seriously considered teaching before—not even while helping Mum with the Girl Guide unit. But the idea glowed on the screen like a neon sign: *This way to adventure.* What if I could trade Excel for tuk-tuks, support tickets for sunrises?

My fingers hovered over the keyboard:

TEFL Thailand. Four-week course. Beachfront. Immediate job opportunities.

And Thailand? Well. That was very tempting.

I'd visited a friend there a few years earlier and fallen head over flip-flops in love with the place. The colors, the chaos, the kindness of strangers—it had all stayed with me. Now here it was again, beckoning like a secret shortcut out of my small, stifling life.

The hum of fluorescent lights overhead and that odd office carpet smell clung to the air. And then I knew, if I didn't do something now—right now—I'd be sitting in this exact seat a year from now, wondering what might've happened if I had.

In a split second, I clicked Apply Now before I could talk myself out of it.

And just like that, I had done it—I became a flight risk. I slumped back in my chair and let out a breath I hadn't even realised I was holding. It was like my soul had been quietly bracing itself, waiting for me to wake up and do something. And I finally had.

I stared at the confirmation screen, heart thudding like I'd just committed a crime. I kept refreshing my inbox until the subject line appeared: *Welcome to your TEFL adventure!*

I had to bite the inside of my cheek to stop from grinning like a maniac. For the rest of the day, I floated somewhere between elation and terror. I'd swing from "this is the best decision of my life" to "what the hell have I just done?" every few minutes. Nobody at work noticed. Maybe I was better at hiding it than I thought. Maybe they were just too deep in their own spreadsheets to see the edges of me lifting.

The rest of the workday passed in slow motion. The seconds ticked by like a narcoleptic snail. But I didn't care. For the first time in what felt like forever, I had something to look forward to. Something that didn't involve toner cartridges or system updates.

That night, I walked home in the drizzle, grinning like a lunatic. Beneath the panic was something else—a pulse of *yes*. For the first time in ages, something inside me had cracked open.

Chapter 3
A Keyring, a One-Way Ticket, and Everything I Didn't Say

I didn't tell anyone at first. Not even Mum. I needed the decision to be mine, if only for a little while.

That week, I began packing in my head, mentally shrinking my life into a 23kg baggage allowance. I sifted through old drawers like an archaeologist, discarding relics of a life I didn't want to carry forward: expired loyalty cards, tangled earrings, birthday cards from people I no longer knew. Each item felt like a choice, a deliberate step toward something new.

When I finally told Mum, she fell silent, her eyes blinking for a moment too long. Then she turned and boiled the kettle, the familiar ritual steadying her. "Thailand?" she said at last, as if I'd announced I was moving to Mars. But then she smiled—a fragile blend of sadness and pride. "Well," she said, stirring her tea, "you've always had itchy feet. I just hoped they'd settle someday."

"I think they're getting itchier," I replied. We both laughed, though my throat tightened with unsaid words.

She didn't try to dissuade me. Instead, she helped me pack up my little house in York, wrapping mugs in newspaper and passing me bubble wrap with quiet efficiency. She moved through the rooms like they were a nest she'd built, dismantling it twig by twig.

"Don't forget your mints," she said suddenly, voice light but her hands slower now. Then she paused, fumbling in the pocket of her cardigan. "And this."

She reached into her pocket and pressed something small and metallic into my palm. It was a keyring—shaped like a tiny silver angel with outstretched wings. I turned it over in my hand, the metal cool against my skin. A lump rose in my throat.

"It's silly," she said quickly, almost brushing it off. "But it might bring you luck and you'll never be alone."

I stared at it for a second too long, blinking hard. "It's not silly," I said. "It's perfect."

She gave me a half-smile, the kind that crumpled at the edges. "I saw it in that little shop on Micklegate. Thought it might keep you safe."

I swallowed, hard. The angel was delicate, worn smooth at the edges. I could picture her choosing it, quietly, on some errand she never mentioned.

She smiled faintly. "Well, you're the one flying off to Thailand with nothing but flip-flops and hope and a prayer."

I looked down at the keyring again. It was just a trinket. But it felt heavier than it should have, like it carried everything we weren't saying.

I didn't trust myself to speak right away. I just nodded and closed my fingers around it like it was something sacred.

"I'll keep it with me," I said, my voice quieter now. "Everywhere I go."

She gave a quick nod, blinking too fast. "Good, Good. Because you might be far away, but you're never going alone, even when you're halfway around the world… I'll still be here. Wondering what you're up to. Hoping you're okay."

And just for a second, I wanted to stop. To sit back down in that half-empty kitchen and rewind everything. But instead, I closed my fingers around the angel and tried to smile.

"I'll call you often," I promised, not knowing if that was even possible.

She gave my arm a squeeze. "I know," she replied, turning away to wrap another glass.

Packing was like flipping through an old diary. Every object carried a memory: the polka dot mug Mum gave me, a stack of unread guidebooks, a drawer stuffed with phone chargers and unfulfilled intentions. Each choice to keep or discard felt like rewriting my story.

I broke the news to others gradually—testing the waters with offhand comments at first, as if I were still trying to convince myself it was real. Some raised sceptical eyebrows; others hugged me like I was heading into battle. A few looked quietly wounded, though they smiled and said they were proud.

My best friends reacted in perfect character.

Diane narrowed her eyes. "Are you sure this isn't some kind of cult? You're not going to end up milking goats on a commune, are you?"

Angela blinked. "Can you even get a refund if it turns out to be a scam? I read this blog post once about a woman who paid for a TEFL course and ended up teaching in a nightclub."

Paul didn't say much at all. Just gave me a long look, took a sip of his pint, and muttered, "You? Thailand?" with a single arched eyebrow, as if I'd announced I was moving to Narnia. But later, when he thought I wasn't looking, I saw him googling "Thailand" on his phone with quiet concentration.

We had a send-off at our usual pub—The King's Arms, with its sticky carpets and wobbly benches and the same dusty jukebox that always skipped during "Bohemian Rhapsody." The air was thick with nostalgia and warm ale and that sense of suspended time you get in a place you've haunted for years.

They made a show of presenting me with a leaving gift: a plastic bag stuffed with what they insisted were "essential items for your new life."

Angela handed me a miniature battery-powered fan. "For when your face melts off."

Diane gave me a tattered second-hand Thai phrasebook with someone else's scribbled notes in the margins. "It's probably outdated, but I liked the handwriting."

Then Paul, grinning like a cat, unveiled a pair of lurid, elephant-print harem pants.

"To help you blend in," he said, deadpan. "Or at least look like every other Brit who's had one too many buckets on Khao San Road."

We laughed until we cried. Or maybe we cried until we laughed. I couldn't tell.

Later that night, as the group began to thin and the jukebox finally managed a full song, Diane pulled me into a long hug. "You're braver than I would be," she whispered. "Don't forget us."

Angela kissed my cheek. "Write everything down. Every ridiculous detail. I want the full travel blog."

Paul just clinked his glass against mine. "You'll be back," he said, but there was something in his voice that made me wonder if he wasn't so sure after all.

As I wandered home that night, tipsy and wrapped in the scent of beer and cigarette smoke and someone's old cologne, I clutched the plastic bag to my chest like a care package from another life. And for the first time, the weight of leaving hit me—not just the adventure ahead, but the strange ache of knowing I wouldn't be here next Friday, laughing in the corner booth, singing badly over chips and cider.

I was trading one world for another. And I didn't know if they'd ever quite fit together again.

When the course details and one-way ticket to Bangkok landed in my inbox, the dream solidified into reality. The fear took shape, but so did the excitement—and it roared louder.

The night before I left, I sat on the edge of a half-deflated air mattress in my empty bedroom, the scuffed walls echoing with absence. My suitcase stood zipped and ready, my passport tucked securely inside. I checked my flight confirmation obsessively, as if it might vanish.

I wasn't fearless. I was terrified. But fear no longer felt like a stop sign. It was a signal—proof that something real was happening, that I was finally, truly about to begin.

I wasn't running away. I was running toward something.

The next morning, a soft northern drizzle shimmered on train tracks, bricks, and even my eyelashes. Mum and I stood on the platform, holding each other too tightly, as if letting go might unravel something we couldn't mend. "I packed you more mints," she said, fussing with my coat collar. "They don't have proper Polos over there, you know."

I managed a watery laugh, my throat too full to speak. Everything felt too full.

When the train doors hissed open, I slung my backpack over one shoulder, my passport zipped inside my coat, the angel keyring nestled in my bag's front pocket. I took a few steps, then turned back. Mum was crying now—quietly, openly. I'd never seen her so unguarded.

"Be brave," she called, her voice catching. "Be brave!"

I nodded, blinking back tears, already halfway gone. I didn't feel brave. I felt like a runaway—not from danger or scandal, but from predictability, from the version of me who might have stayed forever just because it was easier.

As the train pulled away, I watched the station blur through the window. Mum shrank smaller and smaller until she was just a woman in a coat, lost in the crowd. My reflection stared back from the glass, unfamiliar. She looked scared, but beneath the fear, something else flickered—hope, or madness, or both.

The airport was another world: polished floors, echoing announcements. I moved through it on autopilot—bag drop, security, gate—my fingers brushing the keyring's cool metal wings for comfort. It felt solid, grounding.

When the plane took off, I watched England dissolve below—fields, towns, rooftops fading into clouds, then light, then sky.

What have I done? What might I become?

I had no answers. But I had movement, air beneath me, and something pulling me forward. For now, that was enough.

Chapter 4
Touchdown in Chaos

The plane doors opened with a soft hiss, and the heat hit me like a body slam. Thick, damp, and unapologetically tropical—it wrapped itself around me before I'd even stepped fully off the jet bridge. My shirt plastered itself to my back within seconds, and each breath felt like inhaling steam. Still, the thrill of being here—of finally stepping into this unknown—kept me grinning despite the sweat..

Suvarnabhumi Airport was a labyrinth of polished floors, duty-free perfume counters, and glowing signs in a language that looked more like art than script. I clutched my backpack tighter, weaving through crowds of tourists, saffron-robed monks, and businesspeople dragging sleek wheeled suitcases. I felt like a child in a grown-up world—wide-eyed, slightly panicked, but weirdly thrilled.

Outside, Bangkok roared to life. Horns blared in tangled traffic. Street vendors shouted over sizzling woks. The scent of lemongrass, petrol, and something suspiciously fishy hung in the humid air. A tuk-tuk whizzed by, neon lights blinking like it had rolled straight out of a nightclub.

I dragged my suitcase to a designated meeting point near the arrivals exit where a laminated sign reading "TEFL Thailand" bobbed above the crowd. A harried-looking Thai woman with a headset and clipboard waved at me. "You are Ellie?" she asked.

"That's me," I nodded, trying not to look like I was already melting.

She directed me to a battered white minibus where two other trainees were already waiting. I slid the door open and was immediately greeted by a burst of air con and the unmistakable smell of spicy snacks.

"Welcome to chaos," said a voice from the back.

I turned to see a woman with wild red curls and a nose piercing, sprawled sideways across the back seat like she'd already claimed the place as her own. She held out a crinkly packet of shrimp chips like a peace offering.

"I'm Jess. You're stuck with me for the next month, apparently." Jess said, her grin half-wild as she thrust the shrimp chips at me. "First rule of Thailand: eat everything, question nothing. You'll survive longer that way."

I laughed, maybe a touch too quickly, and accepted the chips like a lifeline. "Ellie. Nice to meet you. And I'll take all the snacks I can get."

I smiled, broad and bright, the way I'd practiced in the mirror before leaving the airport. Open. Easygoing. Unbothered.

Inside, my stomach was making small, nervous flips—the kind you can't tell if are excitement or panic. I climbed aboard, Jess straightened up a little. The chips crunched loudly between my teeth, salty and strange, but I kept chewing like this was all perfectly normal. Like I'd done this sort of thing before. Like I wasn't sitting in a stuffy minibus, surrounded by strangers, wondering if I'd just made the biggest mistake of my life.

Jess nudged me with her elbow. "You look like you're faking it just slightly less than the rest of us."

I snorted. "Good. That's the vibe I'm going for. Mildly convincing."

She grinned again, wider this time. "Stick with me. I've got a whole bag of bizarre snacks and questionable advice."

And just like that, something in my chest eased—a notch. Not all the way. But enough.

The van filled up over the next hour as more trainees trickled in. There was a guy in a button-down shirt who looked like he'd wandered away from a finance meeting, a pair of American college students in matching tie-dye, and someone who immediately started filming everything on a GoPro strapped to his chest.

The GoPro guy swivelled his camera toward me, muttering, "Day one, new blood," like I was part of his personal documentary. Jess caught my eye and smirked—a silent promise we'd survive the eccentrics together.

As we pulled away from the airport and the city unfolded outside the window, I rested my forehead against the cool glass. Skyscrapers rose like gleaming fingers against the hazy sky, tangled power lines snaked across intersections, and golden shrines peeked out from behind crumbling concrete walls. I stared, wide eyed, watching Bangkok's neon jungle flick by..It was everything and nothing like the travel blogs had said. My stomach fluttered—half from exhaustion, half from the realization that this was real. No turning back now

We reached the guesthouse well after dark. It was basic but clean, with flickering fluorescent lights and fans that whirred like helicopters. The room was a box of faded blue walls and a single bulb casting long shadows. I showered quickly—more to rinse off the travel weariness than anything else—and collapsed onto the hard mattress. But my brain buzzed with overstimulation. I pulled out my notebook, flipped to a blank page, and started to write.

"Bangkok feels like being born again—but with sweatier clothes. Everything smells different, sounds louder, looks brighter. I have no idea what I'm doing. And yet... I've never felt more certain that I'm exactly where I'm meant to be."

I dropped the pen, turned off the lamp, and lay staring at the ceiling fan spinning lazily above me. In the stillness of the room, the fan rattled like it might take flight, stirring the muggy air without cooling it. Tomorrow, we would travel to Ban Phe and I'd begin the TEFL course that had already upended my life.

But tonight? I was in Thailand. And I wasn't dreaming.

Chapter 5
Ban Phe Bootcamp

The following morning, I woke to a gecko chirping somewhere in the ceiling and the unmistakable sound of Bangkok traffic launching into its daily frenzy. Outside my window, the street had already erupted into life—motorbikes zipping past with entire families balanced on them, vendors setting up carts stacked high with fruit I couldn't name, and music blaring from a shop that may or may not have been selling karaoke equipment.

By 9 a.m., we were herded back into the van, our group now complete. I counted twelve of us: a ragtag bunch of hopefuls armed with backpacks, travel mugs, and the kind of bright-eyed optimism usually reserved for the first day of summer camp.

Our driver—whose name may have been Somchai, though he never officially introduced himself—navigated the roads with the confidence of someone who had definitely seen it all. He cheerfully ignored all lane markings and overtook anything slower than a missile.

I sat next to Jess again, who'd quickly become my comfort person. She had the kind of chaotic, magnetic energy that made you feel like you'd known her for years, even if she'd just stolen the last mini banana from the guest house buffet.

"So," she said between sips of suspiciously sweet coffee, "on a scale of one to complete mental breakdown, how are you feeling?"

"Somewhere between mild existential dread and irrational excitement."

"Perfect. That's exactly where you're supposed to be."

We shared a grin as the city gave way to countryside—concrete replaced by rice paddies, roadside shrines, and the occasional wandering cow. As the air grew saltier, and I caught glimpses of glittering ocean through the trees, a strange calm washed over me. We were almost there.

Ban Phe turned out to be a sleepy coastal town with one main street, a scattering of seafood restaurants, a ferry pier to Koh Samet, and a handful of curious stray dogs who clearly ran the place.

Our accommodation was a low-rise guesthouse just minutes from the beach. It had cold tile floors, humming ceiling fans, and beds that could double as yoga blocks—but it felt like home. Jess and I were assigned to share a room, which she immediately claimed half of by strewing sarongs, shoes, and a small collection of crystals across the furniture.

That afternoon, we were ushered into the training centre—a whitewashed building with plastic chairs, giant fans, and a small reception desk manned by a Thai woman with a strict bun and an even stricter expression.

"Welcome," said a tall woman with cropped blonde hair and the kind of voice that made you sit up straight. "I'm Anya Reed, your lead instructor. Some of you think you've come on holiday. I'm here to inform you: you're wrong."

Someone in the back coughed. Jess whispered, "Bet she eats grammar errors for breakfast."

Anya continued, her tone steely but not unkind. "This course is intense. You'll be up early. You'll be thrown into classrooms before you feel ready. And you will be pushed outside your comfort zones daily. But if you let it, this experience will change you."

It felt like she was looking directly at me when she said it.

Introductions followed. There was Dan, a recently-divorced former paramedic from Birmingham who said he was here to "find himself, or at least find decent coffee." Zoe and Matt, the American gap-year twins who finished each other's sentences and wore matching ankle bracelets. Trevor, a Canadian retiree who thought "grammar" was a woman Anya worked with. And Maeve, an Irish artist who wore kaftans, refused to kill mosquitoes, and referred to teaching as "a spiritual performance."

By the end of the session, I had learned three things:

1. No one really knew what they were doing.
2. Jess and I were definitely going to get in trouble for whispering.
3. I was going to like it here.

Later that evening, a few of us wandered down to the beach, where the sun was bleeding into the horizon like a dropped bottle of orange ink. The ocean lapped lazily at the shore, and someone had rigged up a Bluetooth speaker playing Bob Marley.

Dan handed me a beer and nodded toward the water. "So. What brought you here, Ellie?"

I shrugged, trying to sum up months of dissatisfaction and a single moment of wild decision-making. "I got bored of waiting for life to happen."

He gave me a look that said *yep, same here*.

Behind us, Jess was enthusiastically trying to teach Zoe how to use a squat toilet using only interpretive dance. Trevor was grilling the local bartender about exchange rates and the best local whisky. It was a strange, mismatched, wonderful little family.

As the stars began to freckle the sky and the breeze lifted my hair, I realised I hadn't checked the time once all day.

For the first time in a long time, I didn't want to be anywhere else.

Chapter 6
Lessons & Laughter

I'd barely finished my breakfast—a slightly soggy banana pancake and instant coffee that could strip paint—when Anya clapped her hands at the front of the training room.

"Today," she said, "you teach."

There was a beat of silence. Somewhere behind me, someone dropped their pen. Jess let out a strangled laugh. "She means, like, *actually* teach?"

"Oh yes," Anya replied, like a Bond villain. "Each of you will be paired up and sent to a local school this afternoon. You have three hours to plan a twenty-minute lesson on any beginner-level topic. We'll be observing."

I stared at her. "Wait, real kids?"

"Live ammunition," said Dan, deadpan.

My partner was Zoe—thankfully the calmer of the tie-dye twins—and we agreed on the classic "Feelings & Emotions" as our topic. Easy, right? I mean, I'd definitely seen cartoons where a smiling sun taught kids how to say "happy."

Zoe and I sat under a fan that kept threatening to fall out of the ceiling and cobbled together a lesson plan involving drawings, a simple matching activity, and some dramatic acting (Zoe volunteered to pretend to cry for "sad," which she was weirdly good at).

By 1 p.m., we were sweating through our shirts in a sweltering minivan on the way to Ban Phe School (โรงเรียนบ้านเพ)—a crumbling but colorful compound with a playground, murals of cartoon elephants, and at least one rooster that appeared to be on staff.

A tiny Thai woman in flip-flops led us through a corridor lined with shoeless children who stared at us like we were alien invaders. In the classroom, thirty expectant faces beamed up at me from rows of wooden desks.

"Just speak slowly," the woman whispered. "And smile. A lot."

Then she left. Just like that.

My heart was hammering. I took a deep breath, flashed my most non-threatening grin, and launched into our lesson.

"Hello! My name is Ellie," I said slowly, waving like a kindergarten mascot. "Today we are learning about… feelings!"

Zoe mimed being excited. The kids erupted in laughter.

For a moment, I forgot to be nervous.

We moved through the emotions one by one, acting them out, drawing faces on the whiteboard. The kids copied everything with delightful chaos. When Zoe did her "angry face," a boy in the front row actually stood up and flexed like the Hulk.

Things were going *suspiciously* well—until a small girl in the second row shouted "HUNGRY!" and half the class followed suit, abandoning the lesson to chant it like a war cry.

Zoe looked at me. "We forgot snacks."

By the time we finished our twenty minutes, the classroom was a swirling mess of drawings, giggles, and a boy pretending to faint from heartbreak. But the kids had learned something. They could now chant "I'm happy!" in unison, even if the delivery was a bit cult-like.

As we walked back to the van, red-faced and giddy, Zoe punched my arm. "You smashed it."

"Barely survived it," I laughed, still half-hypnotised by the chaos.

"Nope. You've got the face for teaching."

I paused. "Is that a thing?"

"Oh yeah. It's somewhere between desperate optimism and total disbelief."

That night, back at the guesthouse, we all gathered at the beach bar to share war stories over mango smoothies and cold beers. Maeve had been proposed to by a five-year-old. Trevor had accidentally taught an entire class to say "Good morrow" like it was the 1700s. Jess got locked in the supply closet and emerged victorious with a roll of stickers and a ruler that said "Sexy Elephant."

But no one had a meltdown. No one quit.

We clinked bottles and declared it a victory.

As the night wore on and people drifted away to bed, I stayed back on the sand, legs stretched out, beer in hand, staring at the moon casting a silver trail over the water.

I'd been terrified. I'd messed up half the lesson. But I'd done it.

I wasn't just surviving here. I was changing.

And maybe, just maybe, I was good at this.

Chapter 7
Magic, Mangoes & Moonlit Misadventures

Our first weekend off arrived like a gift from the travel gods. After long days of phonics drills, whiteboard battles, and sweaty schoolyards, the promise of sand and sea was irresistible. The plan was simple: Koh Samet or bust.

We crammed ourselves and our backpacks into a rumbling songthaew bound for the pier, all sunscreen, tangled limbs, and delirious excitement.

The ferry to Koh Samet was overcrowded and rust-streaked, chugging its way across the turquoise Gulf like a defiant little beetle. But the moment we had boarded, the world shifted. As the mainland slipped away behind us, so too did the pressure of the TEFL course. For the first time in what felt like weeks, we could just *be*. I stood at the railing, the salt spray clinging to my skin, wind tugging at my hair as Ban Phe slowly disappeared behind us. The others lounged on the benches nearby, already passing around cans of Chang at ten in the morning like it was perfectly normal.

"I swear," Jess said, fanning herself with a flip-flop, and dragging my attention away from the sea to her "if this island doesn't have a hammock and a bar within five metres of the sea, I'm going to lose my mind."

I laughed, though something twisted quietly in my chest. Her accent—warm and unmistakably American—was oddly comforting. But when Koh Samet appeared on the horizon appeared on the horizon like a mirage—turquoise water, sand so white it almost glowed, and coconut palms swaying —I felt something shift inside me. Something loosening, softening.

Our accommodation was a row of bamboo bungalows strung together like beads on a necklace. The walls were thin enough to hear your neighbor sneeze, but we didn't care. We were islanders now.

That first evening was a blur of cocktails in coconuts, bonfires on the beach, and fire dancers spinning flames like sorcerers. Maeve lost a flip-flop and found a Swedish poet. Jess declared herself a "sea witch" and tried to befriend a crab. I floated somewhere in the middle of it all, barefoot and smiling, letting the night wrap around me like warm silk. I caught myself grinning too much, my limbs heavy with sun and rum and a joy I hadn't felt in ages. When we all collapsed onto beach mats at two in the morning, howling with laughter at someone's awful karaoke version of "Wonderwall," I realised what had shifted in me earlier that day—I felt young again. Not just young in age, but young in spirit, in possibility.

The next day, I woke up to birdsong and the sound of waves lapping lazily at the shore. I wandered alone along the beach, the soft putty-like sand beneath my feet, every step felt like a dream. I was drawn by the scent of mangoes and something faintly mystical in the air.

I found a tiny stall tucked under a crooked palm tree, run by a weathered old woman with a bandana and a toothy grin. Her mango sticky rice was the best I'd ever tasted—sweet, creamy, and just a little bit magical.

After breakfast, I meandered further inland along a trail lined with giant ferns and chirping geckos. That's where I stumbled upon her: a Kiwi named Marla, self-proclaimed "intuitive reader and healer," who was meditating barefoot in a circle of crystals on a shaded patch of sand.

"You've got the glow," she said, opening one eye. "You're on the edge of something big."

"Like sunstroke?" I joked, but something about her expression made me pause.

"No," she said with a knowing smile. "Like transformation. Your aura is practically buzzing."

I laughed, mostly to shake off the weird feeling that she could see straight through me. But I carried her words with me for the rest of the day, like a secret charm.

Later in the day I met the others, but didn't share my strange encounter. We snorkelled in shallow bays, our laughter echoing off the rocks, salt drying on our shoulders. I found myself relaxing and chatting about all sorts really opening up—to Jess, to Matt with his sea-bleached curls, even to Dan, who I'd thought was a bit intense at first, but who now shared some green curry and rice with in companionable silence.

Later, at sunset, I sat alone on the beach, the sand still warm under my feet, the sea turning to glass under a sky streaked with gold and fire. I reflected on what the kiwi woman had told me. I did feel on the edge of something — suspended between two lives—one I'd left behind, and one I hadn't quite fully stepped into. A tiny crab scuttled past me and vanished into its hole, and I thought about how I, too, had crawled into a new kind of being.

That night, everything felt different.

We lit paper lanterns on the beach. One by one, we sent our hopes into the sky. When it was my turn, I hesitated, holding the lantern close. *What do you want, Ellie?* The question buzzed in my chest louder than the cicadas.

I let it go.

The lantern rose slowly, wobbling at first, then catching a breeze and floating up—bright and orange and full of maybe. I watched until it disappeared into the stars, a tiny, flickering speck of courage.

The air was thick with possibility. Maeve and Jess were dancing barefoot in the sand, while I sat beside Zoe, watching the stars and the lanterns reflect off the water.

"You ever feel like you've stepped out of your old life and into someone else's?" I asked.

Zoe handed me a beer. "All the time. Isn't it amazing?"

It was. And terrifying. And exactly what I'd needed.

Back at the bungalow, I couldn't sleep. I lay under the mosquito net, listening to the night—waves, insects, the echo of laughter somewhere down the beach. My skin was tight with salt and sun, but my heart… my heart felt cracked open.

This weekend hadn't just been a break from training. It was something else. A turning point. A quiet beginning.

I wasn't just running away anymore.

I was starting to become someone new.

When we ferried back to Ban Phe the next morning, our sunburnt crew was quieter but content. Something had shifted. We weren't just TEFL trainees anymore—we were adventurers, island escapees, mystic believers, mango devourers.

And though I didn't know it yet, the real transformation—the one Marla hinted at—was still waiting for me. Back in Bangkok. In a tailor's shop that smelled faintly of cedar and fate.

Chapter 8
Farewells & Fittings

The final week of the course arrived in a blur of lesson plans, last-minute grammar revisions, and emotional goodbyes to our students. We were seasoned now—sunned, freckled, a little wiser—and standing in front of a classroom no longer made me want to run for the nearest tuk-tuk.

On our last teaching day, my class surprised me with a handmade card—drawings of cats and cartoon suns, scribbled notes in crooked English, and one big sparkly "Thank you Teacher Ellie" in rainbow crayon. I stared at it, blinking back the sting in my eyes.

"Teacher, you happy?" asked Nan, one of the shyest girls in the group, fiddling with a pink scrunchie.

I smiled through the lump in my throat. "So happy," I said. "You all made my day."

She beamed and ran off to join the others, who were now chanting the days of the week to the tune of "Twinkle Twinkle." I let myself laugh, even as my chest tightened. Who knew a bunch of ten-year-olds could melt your heart just by remembering to add an *s* to "likes"?

The TEFL graduation was modest but electric—plastic chairs beneath a sagging banner, lukewarm punch in paper cups, and certificates exchanged with sweaty handshakes, but the mood was electric. We'd done it. We'd all taken that leap, faced the fear, and landed—however clumsily—on our feet.

"Who would've thought?" Jess whispered to me as we clutched our certificates, still damp from the humidity. "Three weeks ago I couldn't tell a past participle from a mango."

"You still can't," I teased, nudging her shoulder. "But your classroom presence is very convincing."

She raised her plastic cup in mock salute. "Here's to faking it till we make it."

That evening, we celebrated like we were invincible. The local beach bar filled with the sound of clinking bottles, spontaneous dancing, and the bittersweet energy of something ending. Someone brought out a paper lantern, and Maeve gave an impromptu (and very slurred) speech while standing on a rickety plastic chair.

"To us," she declared, wobbling precariously. "To warrior educators! May your board markers never run dry and your students always remember the bloody third person singular!"

We roared with laughter, cheering and clapping like it was a TED Talk.

Jess somehow got hold of a ukulele and serenaded us with a parody of "I Will Survive," reworked entirely with grammar references.

"At first I was afraid, I was petrified…
Kept thinking I could never teach without my verb guide by my side…"

She strummed with exaggerated passion, pausing dramatically to sweep her hair back like a rock star.

"I spent so many nights just marking where they went all wrong,
But I grew strong—*I learned the past perfect tense was long!*"

By the time she pointed directly at me for the chorus—
"I will survive! As long as I've got whiteboard pens, I know I'll stay alive…"
—I nearly fell off my stool laughing.

The whole bar joined in by the second verse, clapping and shouting over the off-key strums. For one glorious moment, we were just a bunch of sleep-deprived, sunburned, grammar-obsessed misfits singing our hearts out on a beach in Thailand.

Later, when the music faded and the group began to scatter into smaller clusters, I wandered down to the shoreline. The air smelled of salt and singed barbecue, and the waves whispered softly at my ankles. I stared out at the dark horizon, waves lapping at my feet like a quiet applause.

I wasn't the same girl who had dragged herself into the fluorescent office at Aviva every morning, secretly dreading the emails, the calls, the grey routine. That girl had been careful. Practical. Quietly heartbroken.

Now… I wasn't sure who I was becoming. But I knew this much: I didn't want to go back.

I closed my eyes and let the warm breeze tangle in my hair. Behind me, someone lit another lantern. It rose slowly into the night sky, casting a soft orange glow before joining the stars.

The universe felt closer here. Like maybe it was listening.

The morning I left Ban Phe, the sun rose slow and syrupy over the sea, casting the sleepy fishing boats in molten gold. I stood outside the training centre one last time, my battered backpack leaning against my leg, heavier now with both souvenirs and stories, and tried to feel ready.

The town was just beginning to stir—scooters humming in the distance, roosters crowing from unseen courtyards, a dog stretching lazily in the shade. Familiar sounds, now. Familiar streets. I knew the woman who sold grilled bananas near the pier. I knew which café had the strongest iced coffee and which 7-Eleven had the dodgy air-con.

Jess emerged from the guesthouse behind me, bleary-eyed but smiling, holding two plastic cups of cold Thai tea.

"For the road," she said, handing me one. "Not that I trust you to get on the right minivan."

I laughed, taking a grateful sip. "I triple-checked the ticket, honest" I paused mentally rechecking everything. "I'm definitely bound for Bangkok. No rogue detours."

"You'll be fine," she said, slinging an arm around my shoulder. "You're basically a professional adventurer now."

I smiled, but my heart was doing that strange flutter again—the kind that hits when something is ending, even if you asked for the ending in the first place.

"I feel like I'm about to step off the edge of a map," I said quietly.

Jess nodded. "Good. That means you're going the right way."

We stood in silence for a moment, watching the sky go from peach to pale blue. A pickup truck rattled past, stacked with watermelons. Somewhere, someone was playing Thai pop through a tinny speaker.

When the minivan finally pulled up in a cloud of dust, I hugged Jess hard, breathing in the familiar mix of coconut sunscreen and mosquito repellent. In that moment, I felt the weight of our shared journey—the late-night grammar debates, the sunburned laughter, the quiet doubts we'd faced together.

"Keep in touch," she said into my shoulder.

"Try and stop me."

I climbed into the van, wedging myself between a suitcase and a monk who gave me a serene nod. As the engine roared to life and Ban Phe began to fall away behind us, I pressed my forehead to the window, watching the palm trees blur past like pages turning. As the road twisted through the country, I dozed against the window, lulled by memories of classrooms, mangoes, and that eerie, wonderful aura reading. Each mile pulled me further from who I'd been—and closer to who I might become.

I didn't know what Bangkok would bring. I didn't know if I'd find work, or love, or even a halfway decent place to live.

But I felt it again—that quiet thrum of courage in my chest. That sense that something was waiting for me.

Not an ending.

A beginning.

Bangkok hit me like a monsoon the moment I stepped off the bus: the smell of fried garlic and motorbike fumes, the heat curling off the pavement, the dizzying pulse of a city that never seemed to sleep. I was back, but I wasn't the same.

I checked into a small guesthouse tucked down a quiet alley off Khao San Road—cheap, clean-ish, and with just enough character to feel like home. The receptionist welcomed me with a shy wai and a room key attached to a plastic mango. I took it as a good omen.

After a quick shower and a cold Chang, I wandered out into the golden chaos of Bangkok's late afternoon. I wasn't sure where I was going, only that I wanted to follow whatever impulse had brought me this far in the first place.

I turned a corner, and that's when I saw it.

A small tailor shop, wedged between a tuk-tuk rental and a place advertising "authentic massage" with suspicious quotation marks. The sign above the door was painted in fading gold script: *Sanjay's Bespoke Tailoring*.

I don't know what made me walk in. Maybe it was the air-conditioning. Maybe it was the universe, gently nudging me toward my next plot twist.

The bell above the door chimed softly as I stepped inside.

It smelled like cedarwood and fresh linen. Rolls of fabric lined the walls—sapphire silks, crisp cottons, earthy linens—all neatly arranged like a painter's palette. At the counter, a man looked up from a measuring tape.

He had dark, thoughtful eyes and a smile that felt like it had been waiting just for me.

"Welcome," he said, his voice warm as summer. "Looking for something special?"

I hesitated, caught by the quiet knowing in his gaze—as if he'd already glimpsed a piece of my story.

"I'm... just browsing," I managed, smiling back.

He nodded, "Sometimes," he said, gently folding a bolt of fabric, "the best things begin that way."

Chapter 9
Suits, Sushi & Surprise Fridges

Bangkok was electric, it was as if the city inhaled me—hot, hectic, relentless. Tuk-tuks zipped by like neon beetles, and everywhere I turned, something was sizzling, honking, or yelling in a language I was still only half-deciphering.

I had applied for countless jobs while finishing the course and now, finally managed to have an interview lined up. In the days leading up to it, I bounced between grimy guesthouses and internet cafés, hunting for work and some semblance of a plan. I wanted to stay. I needed to stay. But I also needed a job that would pay more than enough for pad Thai and a room that had more than cockroaches and paper-thin walls.

When I finally landed an interview at a place called Siam Computer and Language, I celebrated with a banana pancake and promptly realised—I had nothing to wear.

So, I wandered past Sanjay's tailor shop again.

He was outside, smoothing a bolt of emerald silk across a mannequin, the tape measure draped like a scarf around his neck. He looked up, did a double-take, and flashed that grin—half amusement, half mischief.

"Back so soon?" he teased, eyes glinting. "You're either stalking me or my air conditioning."

"Definitely the AC," I shot back, clutching my mango smoothie to hide my flush. He chuckled, flicking his tape measure down from his neck with a slick ease.

I stared.

There he stood with quiet confidence, his slim-fitting shirt contouring his lean frame with effortless precision. The fabric hugged his chest and shoulders, hinting at a physique shaped by years of careful work—strong, but refined. With a grin that managed to be both confident and kind.

I jolted myself back, "I need a miracle," I admitted.

He chuckled and ushered me in with a theatrical sweep of his arm. "Then, you've come to the right place allow me to cool you down and tempt you with Italian linen."

The shop was refreshingly cool, scented faintly of cedar and aftershave, and absolutely out of my budget. But I told him my story—half self-deprecating, half desperate—and instead of showing me the door, Sanjay pulled out a bolt of navy-blue fabric and said, "One-day turnaround. Just promise me you'll ace the interview."

There was an ease between us, the kind that only happens when flirtation feels like a shared secret. He poured me a glass of something cold and fizzy from a fridge hidden behind a wall of suits, and we sat among fabrics and threads like two kids hiding in a fort.

The next morning, I was striding through central Bangkok in my brand-new tailored suit, feeling halfway like a boss and halfway like a fraud. My shoes—bargain bin specials—didn't share my confidence. One heel gave out dramatically near Victory Monument, sending me lurching into traffic with a yelp and a splatter of iced coffee.

I hobbled the rest of the way, blouse sticking to my back, bag slipping off my shoulder, heart thudding in my throat. It wasn't exactly the poised entrance of a seasoned educator, but I was oddly calm. Something had shifted. I didn't panic—I laughed. The girl who'd once dreaded Aviva's fluorescent monotony would've crumbled; but I'd survived Ban Phe's classrooms and Bangkok's chaos, I'd made it this far. The city hadn't spat me out yet.

And somehow, in that sweaty, lopsided state, I delivered a grammar demo on *telling the time* that had the interviewers in fits.

"This is the most entertaining lesson we've seen all week," one of them said, dabbing tears from her eyes. "You just proved you can keep going no matter what."

And just like that—I got the job.

Teaching in Bangkok was its own kind of beautiful chaos. Each day brought a new surprise: cheeky toddlers who high-fived me with sticky hands, teenage monks in saffron robes, retirees who treated our classes like a tea party. One of them, Khun Naree—a glamorous, no-nonsense woman with a bouffant and a fierce streak—latched onto me with alarming affection.

"You're too skinny," she tutted after our first lesson, handing me a bag of mango and sticky rice. "You need sushi. Good sushi. I take you, you need anything? I get for you."

I thought she was joking—until the following week, when she pulled up outside the language centre in a battered pickup truck and hollered my name like she was in that limousine scene from Pretty Woman

"Ellie! Come! I bring something!"

It was a fridge.

"I heard your apartment is empty. This is not new, but you need it. Teacher must not get sick!"

I blinked. "Wait—seriously?"

She beamed. "Of course. You are my friend."

From then on, our lessons spilled out of the classroom. "We practise English in real life," she declared, dragging me through malls, markets, and food courts.

"What if I am a rich lady who forgot her Thai?" she said one day, dramatically fanning herself. "You must help me survive!"

I played along, helping her haggle in English over handbags and order bubble tea. She laughed, I learned, and somewhere along the way, I stopped feeling like an outsider and started feeling like I belonged.

The rest of my days unfolded like a documentary on the contradictions of Thai society. I taught everyone from pre-schoolers in Spider-Man T-shirts to sharply dressed business executives to softly spoken sex workers who shyly practised restaurant English. I never knew what to expect—but I knew I loved it.

On weekends, I became a traveller again—riding buses into the unknown of the national nature reserves, hiking to waterfalls with my flip-flops in hand, watching monkeys leap through jungle canopies and wondering how my life had become so unrecognisably full.

I didn't have much money, and so, drawn by the vibrancy of the place I would spend many evenings along Khaosan Road—a place full of colorful characters and crazy stories. I met a Dutch juggler with a pet ferret named Coconut, a retired Australian who swore he'd been abducted by aliens, and once, a Canadian backpacker who offered to tattoo my name in Thai script on his calf after three Chang beers. I told him to sleep on it.

My world had cracked open in a thousand directions, and instead of feeling lost—I felt alive.

Bangkok was beginning to feel like mine. The chaos no longer overwhelmed me—it energised me. Each morning I'd dive into the current, riding the Skytrain with office workers, monks, and teenagers scrolling on cracked phones, feeling like a thread in the city's impossibly vivid fabric.

I'd sometimes pass Sanjay's shop and wave. Once or twice I stopped in just to say hi, to sip tea and talk about nothing. He always made time, and he always smiled like he was glad to see me.

At the time, I told myself it was just friendship. That he was just kind.

There was ease now. Familiarity. I talked about how Ban Phe felt like a dream, and how Bangkok was everything and too much all at once. He told me how the shop was handed down from his uncle, and how tailoring in this city was part skill, part survival.

"And part theatre," he added, grinning, "especially with customers like you."

I gasped in mock offence. "Excuse you, I am a consummate professional. I've only ruined *one* suit."

"That I know of."

The banter danced between us, effortless.

It started like that—visits after school, drinks around the corner, teasing banter that danced right up to the edge of something more

"You look… like you belong here," he said quietly, smoothing the fabric at my shoulder.

I met his gaze, heart thudding a little faster. "Some days, I think I do."

There was a pause—not awkward, but full. A possibility hanging there between the tailor's tape and the hum of the city beyond the shop door.

"You should come out with me sometime," he said at last. "Not as a customer."

I smiled. "I'd like that."

And just like that, another thread stitched itself into the strange, beautiful tapestry of my new life.

We met outside the Asok BTS station on a Thursday evening—early enough that the sky still glowed pink, but late enough for the traffic to start its nightly opera of horns and motorbike rumbles.

Sanjay looked freshly pressed, as always. Crisp white shirt, cuffed jeans, leather loafers that made me feel instantly underdressed in my sandals and long skirt that had definitely seen better laundry days. Still, he smiled like I was the best thing he'd seen all week.

"I thought we'd skip the usual expat haunts," he said. "There's a little rooftop place nearby. Good food. Even better view."

"I'm in," I said, trying to sound breezy and not like my heart was doing backflips.

The bar was perched above a crumbling colonial building, all fairy lights and whispering faded grandeur. We climbed a narrow stairwell that smelled like old incense and hot concrete, emerging onto a rooftop strung with fairy lights and faded paper lanterns. The city sprawled out in every direction—glittering towers piercing the sky, tangled wires crisscrossing like veins, and in the distance the Chao Phraya River catching the day's last blush.

Over plates of paneer tikka and mango salad, we traded stories. I told him about my disastrous demo lesson and the broken heel. He told me about the time a client fainted during a fitting because he'd skipped lunch and got too excited about Italian wool.

"Do you miss England?" he asked at one point, after we'd laughed ourselves hoarse over a shared tale of Bangkok plumbing failures.

"Less than I thought I would," I admitted, toying with a basil leaf. "There are moments—when I see a proper kettle, or walk past somewhere that smells like toast—but mostly? I feel like I'm becoming someone else here. Someone braver."

He tilted his head. "I can see that. You've got this... spark. Like you're figuring out how to be exactly where you're meant to be."

I blinked, caught off guard by the gentleness in his voice.

"You always this charming?" I asked, half joking, half hoping.

"Only on Thursdays," he replied, raising his glass of lemon soda.

We clinked glasses. Mine fizzed over and dripped onto the table. Of course.

He grinned. "There she is."

After dinner, he ordered us cocktails with names like *Bangkok Blues* and *Ginger Sling*, and we talked for hours—about cities we'd loved, childhoods in wildly different worlds, and dreams neither of us had shared out loud before.

He told me he'd grown up in Myanmar, moving to Bangkok for his uncle's shop, and staying for the city's chaotic charm. "Bangkok's full of secrets," he said, his voice softening. "Just when you think you know it, it reveals something strange and beautiful—like you."

I blushed. He reached across the table and tucked a strand of hair behind my ear.

After dinner, we wandered without direction. Past food stalls and neon signs, old men playing chess in front of 7-Elevens, and monks buying bottled water in orange robes that glowed under the fluorescent lights. Everything felt a little surreal. Or maybe just perfectly alive.

We paused on a pedestrian bridge overlooking a stream of red taillights.

"So," he said, glancing sideways, "what happens next for you?"

I exhaled. "I'm not sure. I've got this job, and an apartment with furniture that doesn't match, and a fridge that a student gave me from the back of a truck. But I wake up most mornings excited. That's new."

He nodded, thoughtful. "That's everything."

He didn't kiss me. Not that night. But his hand brushed mine as we said goodbye, fingers lingering just a second too long. And I walked away into the Bangkok night with a smile I couldn't quite hide.

Something was unfolding—quietly, stitch by careful stitch. And for once, I wasn't afraid to see where the pattern would lead.

Soon, we were weaving into each other's lives. He'd bring lunch to my school; I'd show up at his shop with iced coffees and stories of kids mispronouncing "zebra." He offered to make me a dress for my sister's wedding in England—"Something light, elegant. Not too English."

He spent hours sketching and pinning and adjusting while I stood barefoot on a pedestal in the back of his shop. When I saw the finished piece—a silk halter dress in the most delicious shade of turquoise—I was speechless.

"It's not just a dress," he said, standing behind me in the mirror. "It's a memory."

I nodded, touched by the care he'd poured into it. "It's perfect."

Our relationship wasn't perfect, he worked long hours. I never quite knew when he was being serious, and sometimes I'd catch myself wondering where, exactly, this was going. But when we were together—trading glances across crowded rooms, cooking street noodles in his tiny kitchen, dancing in the glow of market lanterns—it felt like we were suspended in time.

Not quite forever. But far from goodbye.

Chapter 10
Behind the Beads

The city throbbed with its usual madness—the air thick with the mingled scents of sizzling street food and diesel fumes, a heady perfume that was both enticing and overwhelming. Laughter spilled from ping pong shows into the sultry night, a cacophony of mirth that mingled with the distant hum of traffic. Glitzy malls, their glass facades shimmering like mirages, loomed over crumbling temples, where faded gold leaf clung to ancient stone. Neon signs bathed the cracked pavement in an otherworldly glow, casting the scene in hues of electric blue and pink. Here, modernity and tradition stood in stark juxtaposition, a testament to Bangkok's ceaseless dance between the sacred and the profane.

One humid evening, after Sanjay had wrapped up his day's work, he turned to me with a cheeky, mischievous smile, his dark eyes twinkling with a secret only he held. Raising an eyebrow, he leaned in and whispered, "There's a hidden gem in this city, a place where the veil between reality and fantasy blurs. Are you brave enough to peek behind the curtain—Nana Plaza?"

"I'm intrigued," I replied, my voice trembling with excited curiosity. My heart raced as my mind conjured images from the whispered tales of backpackers—those knowing grins and raised eyebrows that mirrored Sanjay's own. I'd never summoned the courage to venture there myself, but with his invitation, the pull was irresistible.

We set off, weaving through a labyrinth of neon-lit alleys where the air pulsed with the rhythm of Thai pop music and the animated chatter of revelers. We slipped past open-air bars, their fluorescent lights flickering like fireflies, dodging expats in cargo shorts who laughed with abandon and locals whose eyes glimmered with untold stories. The unsteady clack of heels on the fractured pavement reverberated around us, blending with the scents of perfume and sweat that hung heavy in the air. A quiet thrill prickled my skin. It could have felt seedy, this nocturnal odyssey, but with Sanjay beside me—calm, amused, a steady presence—it was as though we'd stepped into a secret pocket of the city, a realm where the ordinary rules dissolved.

Tucked into a shadowed corner of Nana Plaza, up a narrow staircase that creaked beneath our feet, we parted a beaded curtain and entered a dim room that enveloped us like a sigh. The air was heavy with the sweet embrace of jasmine and the earthy whisper of sandalwood, a fragrance that wove a spell of intimacy. The clamour from below softened to a distant throb, as if the city itself had paused to breathe. This small bar was a sanctuary—velvet cushions adorned low tables, their deep hues catching the flicker of candlelight from colored glass jars. Incense curled lazily toward the ceiling, and a smoky hush settled over us, laced with the cool hum of anticipation.

All of that faded the moment the stage ignited with light and the music began. My gaze was drawn to the centre of the room, where a rotating, tiered platform rose like a glossy white wedding cake, bathed in washes of pink and blue. The music started soft and teasing, a hypnotic whisper that swelled into a pulse, drawing every eye. From the wings, they emerged—performers materializing like apparitions, each a masterpiece of transformation and allure. Some towered in stilettos, their lashes long and curves sculpted, every movement a symphony of elegance and power. Others glided with fluid, enigmatic grace, blurring the boundaries between masculine and feminine, reality and dream, as if they inhabited a space beyond definition.

I watched, wide-eyed, not with judgment, but with awe.

"They're like… living poems," I whispered to Sanjay, my voice barely audible over the music, my eyes unable to break away. "Each one a testament to the power of self-creation."

He nodded, his gaze fixed on the stage, a quiet reverence in his expression. "Their beauty is hard-won," he murmured. "A testament to their resilience and artistry. They are warriors of the stage, battling for their place in the spotlight."

There was no trace of shame in his tone—only deep admiration.

Sanjay ordered drinks with the ease of a regular, sliding a glass toward me with a brush of his fingers against mine. "This place is an eye-opener," he said, his voice low and intimate, resonating with the room's smoky hush. "Many never find it. That's kind of the point."

I took a sip—sweet, sharp, spiced with an exotic note I couldn't name, much like the city itself. Leaning closer, I teased, "So, is this where you bring all your clients?"

He chuckled, a soft rumble that sent a shiver down my spine. "Only the ones who show up barefoot and asking for a miracle," he shot back, his eyes sparkling with mischief.

"Fair," I conceded, a smile tugging at my lips despite myself.

On stage, a siren clad in sequins seized the spotlight, her voice a haunting echo of heartbreak and hope as she lip-synched a ballad. Each note pierced the soul, her fierce grace sending chills across my skin. Another performer enacted a breakup scene, peeling away layers of costume to reveal a glimmering bodysuit beneath, as if shedding heartbreak itself in a cascade of light. Between acts, they floated through the crowd like ethereal beings, collecting compliments, drinks, and tips—sometimes more. Their beauty was magnetic, but it was the effort beneath—the invention of self, the artistry, the resilience—that struck me most.

As I savoured my cocktail, the lines of my old life—my IT desk, the dreary English drizzle, my endless hesitation—blurred further into oblivion. The mundane trappings of that former existence felt like a distant dream, supplanted by the vibrant, chaotic reality of this neon-lit wonderland. I was no longer a mere observer; I was woven into the fabric of this bright, unrepeatable strangeness.

"Bangkok," Sanjay murmured, his breath warm against my ear, "will show you everything—if you're willing to look."

We lingered for hours, our voices hushed beneath the music, time stretching out like warm molasses. At some point, his hand found mine across the table, his warm fingers curling tenderly around mine in a gentle squeeze. No words—just a steady touch that sent a soft shiver through me, unexpected and disarming. It was the gentlest gesture, and it caught me utterly off guard. My heart lurched, a clumsy echo of adolescent flutters long forgotten.

It wasn't romance in the grand, obvious sense—no sweeping declarations or cinematic kisses—but the evening carried a slow, deliberate *yes*. A permission. A beginning.

Later, we emerged from the bar's cocoon into the embrace of the humid night, neon lights painting our path in electric hues. My heels dangled from my fingers—I'd abandoned them halfway through the night—and Sanjay slipped his arm around my shoulders as we walked. We laughed until our stomachs ached, the kind of laughter born from exhaustion and an overwhelming sense of being alive.

At the edge of the plaza, beside a food stall wafting the aroma of midnight noodles, he paused and turned to me. The streetlight caught his face—half shadow, half something tender, like a promise etched in light.

He tucked a damp strand of hair behind my ear, his touch lingering. "You alright?" he asked, his voice soft as the night.

"Yeah," I breathed, barely above a whisper. "I didn't expect any of that."

He smiled, the corners of his eyes crinkling. "Good. Thailand's full of things you don't expect."

Then, without fanfare, he drew me closer in the shadow of a flickering streetlamp, his lips meeting mine in a kiss that was both a question and an answer. Soft, hesitant, it tasted faintly of spice and the night's adventures—not cinematic, no swelling orchestra, just a shy, impossibly real moment. Yet it carried weight, a subtle shift in the world's axis, enough to know I'd never see things quite the same.

Hand in hand, we surrendered to the city's embrace, the memory of that night a secret talisman folded quietly between us—a reminder that magic could bloom in the most unexpected places.

Chapter 11
Between Worlds

By midweek, I was halfway through a lesson on animal sounds with a room full of five-year-olds when I realised, I'd stopped checking the clock.

I'd fashioned paper ears for everyone—lions, cows, ducks—and we were crawling around the classroom mooing, quacking and roaring. One child—wildly enthusiastic—scaled my leg, shrieking like a monkey.

"Okay, okay! Everyone freeze!" I laughed, holding up the giant plastic clock we used for time lessons. "What time is it when the lion roars?"

A sea of giggles.

"Snack time!" shouted one tiny girl in pigtails, clutching her lion mask upside down.

Not quite what I was going for—but she wasn't wrong.

The chaos didn't faze me anymore. Somewhere between the classroom chaos and late-night Bangkok adventures, I'd crossed a threshold—I wasn't just surviving Thailand, I was thriving. Improvising, laughing, learning, flailing at times—but doing it. And weirdly, joyfully, it was starting to feel like home.

At lunch, I sat in the shade outside the centre with a plastic tub of rice and spicy stir-fried basil, watching the world tilt lazily by. Sanjay had sent me a text that morning: *Dinner later? I found a rooftop place you'll love. Dress comfortably. And bring that laugh I like.*

I couldn't stop smiling at my phone.

The relationship had crept up on us—not in a blaze of passion, but with a kind of steady warmth. Sanjay wasn't just charming; he was patient, funny, absurdly insightful, and unbothered by my frequent tendency to monologue about minor cultural crises or the dramatic highs and lows of my teaching days.

He always listened. Then handed me mango slices like it was a cure-all.

That afternoon, I checked my email and squealed—loud enough to startle the teacher's lounge.

Subject: Flights booked!
From: Diane 👯
"We're coming!! Me, Angela and Paul—all flights confirmed. We land in Bangkok three weeks today. Prepare for chaos. And probably sunburn. Also, we expect pad thai on arrival. And maybe a tuk-tuk with our names painted on the side. LOVE YOU."

I clutched the phone to my chest like a teenage girl in a '90s rom-com.

After weeks of navigating it all solo—leaking AC units, exploding whiteboard markers, a student who liked to answer everything with "Spaghetti!"—the idea of seeing my people again was both surreal and grounding. They knew the version of me before all this. The pub-after-work, dating-disasters, Ellie-who-burned-toast version. And now they'd see this version—sun-kissed, standing barefoot in classrooms, kissing tailors on rooftops, figuring it all out one improvised lesson at a time.

The city roared below. Bangkok never really stopped. For the first time, I felt still—my breath steady against the city's roar, as if I'd finally found my place in its pulse.

I had no idea what was coming next, but I wasn't afraid of it anymore.

When Diane and Angela touched down in Bangkok, everything felt a little louder, a little lighter. Their arrival jolted me into an old rhythm—the shorthand jokes, the shared glances, the British sarcasm that had no translation. They came armed with Cadbury's and dry shampoo, marvelled at my growing tan and fluent-sounding Thai, and immediately started sweating in the tropical heat. Paul joined a few days later, all banter and backpack bravado. He cracked jokes about the tuk-tuks, ordered the spiciest curries on menus just to prove a point, and flirted outrageously with every smiling waitress who came within a metre. Seeing them was both comforting and disorienting. Their reactions to Bangkok mirrored my own first impressions—chaotic, colorful, slightly absurd—but I no longer saw it that way. I'd stopped flinching at sidewalk rats and motorbikes on pavements. I'd become part of the rhythm.

One night, I brought them to meet Sanjay. We arranged to meet at a rooftop bar in Silom, just as the sun began to slide down behind the skyline. Sanjay arrived last, effortlessly stylish in a linen shirt and pressed trousers, a stark contrast to our mismatched tourist wear. He brought with him the kind of smooth charm only Bangkok locals seemed to master—equal parts gracious host and effortless insider. "Welcome to my city," he said with a mock bow, handing Paul a Chang beer and sliding a mango cocktail toward Angela. "You've chosen the right tour guide, you know. Ellie is practically Thai now." The evening unfolded like a film. Sanjay led us to a tiny backstreet restaurant—no menu, just steaming bowls of noodles and grilled pork skewers served on plastic tables. He taught us how to toast properly in Thai ("chon!") and to say aroi mak mak for "very delicious,", shared funny stories about tailoring for Bangkok's most eccentric expats, and playfully teased me in front of everyone, making the girls giggle and Paul raise an eyebrow. Over beers and laughter, Sanjay told the story of the time a Russian groom ordered a dozen identical tuxedos for his twelve near identical cousins and encouraged Paul to try a fried cricket—just for the story. Paul did, naturally, and regretted it halfway through chewing. But when my friends flew back home, something shifted again. The energy dipped, like a stage after the final bow. I was left with their half-used sunscreen, echoing laughter, and a renewed awareness of the space I now occupied—one foot in Bangkok, one foot in the memory of who I'd been.

A month later, my sisters Cristina and Jenny arrived in Bangkok, straight from Heathrow. I met them at their hotel—an old, faded boutique place near Phra Athit Road with a rooftop that promised river views but mostly delivered the scent of exhaust and lemongrass. Cristina was already fussing with the air-conditioning remote when I knocked. Jenny opened the door, eyes wide, cheeks flushed from the heat, hair in a lopsided ponytail. She beamed when she saw me.

"Ellie!" she said, stepping forward and nearly tripping over her suitcase strap.

I caught her just in time, hugging them both in a tangle of limbs and jetlag. It was surreal, seeing them in this world of mine—so familiar to me now, so utterly alien to them.

Cristina, as expected, had come prepared. She'd printed out maps, bookmarked blogs, and had a list of "must-sees" that she'd color-coded by neighborhood. Jenny, sweet and a little uncertain, had brought a mosquito net she didn't know how to use, three different sun creams, and an openness to pretty much anything—as long as someone else made the plan.

The first few days were a blur of exploration. We stood in awe beneath the towering spires of Wat Arun, wandered through the endless maze of Chatuchak Market, and got completely derailed during a foot massage in a dingy back alley that left us all limping and shrieking with laughter. Jenny had to lie down afterwards, claiming she wasn't entirely sure her legs still worked.

Jenny gripped my arm in the tuk-tuk, squealing, 'We're gonna die!' at every turn, then whispering, 'Sorry, so sorry,' as she slipped the driver a crumpled baht note. "Sorry! I'm so sorry!" became her catchphrase, though they usually just laughed and waved us off.

Cristina kept us moving, but Jenny kept us light.

After a few days of temples, sweat, and sensory overload, I proposed we escape to the place where my Thailand journey had begun—Koh Samet. They agreed without hesitation.

The bus ride south was bumpy but manageable. The speedboat that followed... less so. The journey was choppy, the sea brilliant turquoise beneath the white hull. I felt the stress peel off in layers with each bounce over the waves. Jenny sat gripping the edge of her seat, knuckles white, mumbling, "Oh God, oh God," with every wave that slapped the hull.

Cristina rolled her eyes. "You'll be fine, Jen."

"I didn't sign up for a rollercoaster on water," Jenny muttered. "If I get flung off..."

And then, with absolutely perfect timing, Jenny stood up to take a photo... and was promptly launched overboard by a rogue swell. There was a collective gasp—then a splash. She screamed. I jumped up, yelling for a life ring, my heart hammering. But then Jenny surfaced, flailing, gasping, and coughing all at once with mascara-streaked cheeks.

"Am I dead?" she gasped. "Did I die?"

Cristina let out a bark of laughter so loud the skipper turned around. The boat looped back. I helped haul her on board, soaked and dripping, her hair plastered to her face.

"Koh Samet: 1, Jenny: 0," I said, handing her a towel and breathing a sigh of relief.

The island greeted us like an old friend—powder-soft sand, clear sea, and beach bars playing lazy reggae tracks. Jenny recovered quickly, soothed by sugary cocktails and the novelty of drinking from a bucket with a neon straw. We swam until dark, floated under a moon so full it felt too perfect to be real. It was the kind of night you never take pictures of, because nothing could capture how perfect it felt.

That night, our skin salty and our hearts light, barefoot and a little buzzed, we lay on the soft, giant, beach chairs, the fire flairs flickering in the soft sea breeze, beneath the stars. Cristina asked gently about Sanjay, about what came next. Jenny joked about moving to Thailand and opening a beach bar with me. And in those moments, I felt the pull of both lives again—the grounding force of family, and the wild, messy freedom I'd found here. I didn't know how to explain the in-between I now lived in, the strange truth that I belonged everywhere and nowhere at once.

Later, after they'd gone to bed—sandy and sun-soaked and half-buzzed on cheap rum—I stayed behind, toes buried in the cool powder of the shore. The tide had come in. The lights of the beach bars flickered behind me like distant memories already forming. Out there in the dark, somewhere past the moonlit waves, was everything I hadn't figured out yet. I thought about Sanjay. About Bangkok. About the classroom chaos, the cracked pavements, the mornings heavy with incense and diesel fumes. I thought about Paul's laughter, Diane's delight, Angela's wide-eyed wonder. About Jenny's shocked face rising out of the water. About how much had changed—inside and out. I used to think this was a phase. A chapter I'd flip past before returning to real life. But maybe this was real life now. The waves whispered at my ankles. I didn't have answers. Just this feeling—contentment, excitement, electric, alive. I hugged my knees, the waves brushing my toes, Sanjay's laugh still echoing in my ears. I wasn't the old Ellie anymore—and I wasn't done becoming this new one.

Chapter 12
Let Go, Begin Again

Thailand had changed me. As my first year abroad drew to a close, I knew I couldn't return to York—to grey mornings, microwave lunches, and the version of myself that sleepwalked through my twenties. A hunger for adventure had taken hold, and though I didn't know where I'd land next, one thing was certain: I wasn't done yet.

The decision to leave Siam Language Centre wasn't easy, but I'd made peace with it—Thailand had given me the TEFL certificate and the travel bug and with it came the thrilling question of where next? Mexico, Europe, China—who knew?

So, I handed in my notice, expecting to work out the month like a professional adult But I hadn't expected to be shown the door so abruptly.

I was mid-way through preparing a lesson on prepositions of place when my Thai supervisor, Mr. Sakchai, appeared in the doorway, shifting awkwardly from foot to foot.

"Ellie… can talk?" Mr. Sakchai said, tapping his watch awkwardly.

In the small office near reception, my stomach knotted. "You finish today," he said, wincing. "Not come back tomorrow."

I blinked, stunned. "What? I thought I had the month."

He shook his head, offering a tight smile. "Company rule. Sorry."

"But I have rent to pay," I stammered. "I need time to—"

"Talk to head office," he interrupted gently. "I not decide."

Tears stung before I could stop them, hot and humiliating.

He shifted again, visibly uncomfortable. "No cry," he said softly, handing me a scratchy tissue from his desk drawer. "Head office. Maybe help."

I nodded, wiping my face, trying to steady my breathing. "Okay. I'll call them."

The call to the head office was patchy, full of static and long pauses, but eventually, I got through to a woman named Noon.

"Yes, we know," Noon said, her tone brisk. "But there's an option."

I sniffled. "Option?"

"A public school program. Weekend event—Family Fun Day. You'd lead English games, music, dancing. Good energy for you, yes?"

It wasn't what I'd expected. I'd pictured a clean break, maybe a new country. But something stirred—a chance to stay, to keep building this life I wasn't ready to leave.

"Yes," I said, voice steadying. "I'll do it."

I walked out of the office in a daze and almost collided with Pat, an older experienced colleague.

"You okay?" she asked, eyeing me with quiet concern.

"Honestly?" I said, blinking back the sting of humiliation. "No. But also… maybe, yeah. I think I am."

She smiled and patted my arm gently. "You will be. This place isn't everything."

She was right. Losing that job was jarring, yes—but also weirdly clarifying. It reminded me that as a foreigner, my position here was always a bit precarious. I wasn't owed anything. I had to keep adapting.

A few days later, the admin team gave me more information. First a spot in a public school outreach programme. "There's a Family Fun Day coming up," said one of the coordinators during a call, "and we need someone to run English games and do a Family Links workshop. It's out in the provinces, a bit rural, but the kids love it. Up for it?"

"What exactly is Family Links?" I asked, suspicious.

"Oh, you know... English bonding stuff. Songs, games, conversations between parents and kids. We'll send you a loose outline."

"Loose?" I repeated. "How loose?"

"You'll be fine!" they chirped.

And just like that, I found myself on a rickety school bus with no air-con, surrounded by excited children and their parents, all chattering in Thai and passing snacks down the aisles like we were on a school holiday. We were headed for a weekend event in a tiny village I'd never heard of, where I was supposed to inspire educational joy through team-building games and tongue twisters.

One of the mums leaned over and offered me a bag of mango slices soaked in chilli and fish sauce. I accepted with both hands, said *khop khun ka*, and braced myself for the taste. It was like a slap and a kiss at the same time.

"You like spicy?" she asked, laughing at my wide eyes.

"I do now!" I managed, fanning my tongue dramatically. The whole row giggled.

As we arrived, the sun dipped behind the rice paddies, painting the fields gold and filling the air with the earthy scent of warm earth and grilled corn. We stayed in a basic guesthouse beside the school, its creaky dorm-style rooms draped with mosquito nets as flimsy as cobwebs. I barely slept—nerves, heat, and the hum of cicadas keeping me awake—but by morning, I was buzzing with anticipation.

The school grounds transformed into a makeshift carnival. Colorful tarps were strung up for shade. Mats were laid out in the courtyard. Someone was grilling sausages near the playground, and music blasted from a tinny speaker: Thai pop songs mashed up with the occasional Western tracks including *Baby Shark* and *YMCA*.

I led a game of English animal charades with a crowd of children aged five to ten. "Who can show me a monkey?" I called, and twenty little bodies began hopping and scratching their heads, shrieking with laughter. Their parents watched from plastic chairs, smiling and occasionally joining in— though one dad took the tiger impression *very* seriously and almost bowled over a row of chairs.

Later, I organised a "Family Spelling Bee," where teams had to act out words instead of spell them. The word "elephant" led to an impressive group effort involving trunk miming, ear flapping, and a spontaneous trumpet sound from a grandma with no teeth.

"Very good!" I cheered. "You win ten imaginary points and a round of applause!"

The kids clapped wildly. One boy shouted, "Khun Ellie, you funny teacher!" and I couldn't stop smiling after that.

In the afternoon, we sang songs under a tree. I taught them "Head, Shoulders, Knees and Toes," which quickly turned into a competitive sport. Then we switched to "If You're Happy and You Know It," and by the time we got to "stomp your feet," even the grumpy teens were laughing.

During the final session, I guided a simple dialogue between parents and children in English:

"My name is…"
"I like…"
"I am proud of you because…"

That last one— "I am proud of you because…"—caught them off guard. A hush fell. Then, slowly, parents turned to their children, whispering halting English: "I proud… you kind," or "I proud… you try hard." A mother's voice cracked; a boy wiped his eyes. I swallowed hard, blinking back my own tears.

Afterwards, one of the teachers came over and said, "You did good. You made the parents feel brave."

I didn't know what to say. I just nodded and looked out at the rice fields, glowing in the late light.

That weekend clarified why I'd come to Thailand: not for job security or escape, but for connection—moments of joy that made people feel seen and capable. On the bus ride home, sticky with sweat and glitter, a little girl leaned against me. "Teacher Ellie, you come again next time, okay?"

"Okay," I said, smiling. "If they let me."

"You funny teacher," she murmured, sleepy.

I wasn't anyone's steady anything anymore. But I was becoming something new—resilient, open, ready for whatever came next.

Chapter 13
Chalk Dust & Changemakers

A wall of noise slammed into me as I stepped into the classroom—thirty-five kids shrieking, giggling, scraping chairs under a squeaky fan that did nothing to cut the heat. Faded Mickey Mouse knock-offs peeled from the walls, and I clutched a stick of chalk, my only weapon. This was my final month in Thailand, diving headfirst into the chaos of its public schools.

The culture shock hit hard: no air conditioning, no fancy tech, just a stick of chalk, a temperamental whiteboard marker, and dozens of sweaty, eager faces staring up at me, expecting answers I didn't have.

I did not have all the answers.

"Okay class," I said on my first day, clapping my hands for attention. "Let's play a game!"

Blank stares.

One boy sneezed with such enthusiasm that he nearly fell off his chair. A girl in the back row had already started plaiting her neighbor's hair.

"Game!" I mimed desperately, tossing a beach ball into the sea of eager faces.

The room exploded—kids chanting "Blue! Red!" and shrieking as the ball thudded to the floor, pure joy in the chaos.

It was messy, hot, and utterly glorious.

Every day brought some small moment of connection. A student who finally pronounced "vegetable" correctly. A shy smile. A carefully folded origami elephant left on my desk.

One morning, I arrived to find the older girls had drawn me a picture. It showed a stick-figure version of me with a giant smile, surrounded by hearts and speech bubbles filled with "Hello! Good morning!" and "I like banana!"

It nearly made me cry.

Teaching in the public schools was exhausting. My clothes clung to me from the moment I stepped off the songthaew. The chalk dust got everywhere. There were days when I'd lose my voice by lunchtime and get home with an aching back and a fried brain.

But it was real. It was meaningful. And strangely, it was healing.

The SCL centre debacle—a volunteer program that collapsed under mismanagement—left me humiliated, questioning why I'd come to Thailand. But here, amid the sweaty chaos, a student's triumphant "vegetable" or a shyly offered origami elephant reminded me why I stayed: for the messy, unpredictable beauty of connection.

One afternoon, I stayed after class to help a group of students practise a little welcome speech in English. The lead boy, Nong Art, kept forgetting his lines and giggling into his palm.

"Try again," I said gently.

He stood straighter. "Good morning! We are happy to learn English with you!"

It was probably the hundredth time he'd said it, but it still made my heart lift. They were trying. I was trying. And that was enough.

During my last week, a teacher handed me a small notebook filled with notes from the kids. Drawings, thank-yous, a few phonetic attempts at "We will miss you Teacher Ellie." I held it to my chest and blinked away tears.

On my final day, a shy girl pressed a tissue paper flower into my hand, her smile brighter than the wobbly "We love Teacher Ellie!" poster behind her. That delicate flower cracked something open in my chest—a certainty that these kids had given me purpose. As I waved from the minivan, clutching it while the school faded in the rearview, I knew: Thailand had taught me I could start over, anywhere, carrying their joy with me.

Thailand had shown me that.

And I wasn't done learning yet.

Chapter 14
Letting Go, Leaping Forward

The fan whirred above, slicing through Bangkok's thick air with a weary rhythm. My once-alien apartment—strange light switches, too-firm mattress—had become a patchwork of memories. The fridge, the one that had arrived in the back of a pickup like something out of a Richard Gere film, stood loyally in the corner, humming along as if it too knew we were nearing the end.

I sat on my bed, phone pressed to my ear, waiting for the familiar ringtone to connect.

"Ellie?" Mum's voice was warm, surprised. "Everything alright?"

I swallowed the lump in my throat. "Yeah. I think… I think I'm coming home."

A pause, then that soft chuckle of hers. "About time. I've just made a shepherd's pie."

I laughed, blinking away tears. "Perfect. I've missed that."

We chatted about flights and weather and how her neighbor had finally trimmed that hedge. But when we said goodbye, and I hung up, I didn't feel like I was going *back*, not really.

Thailand had cracked me open, filled me with stories and faces I'd never forget. Home wasn't a postcode or tea with two sugars anymore—it was a feeling: curiosity, connection, freedom.

Clothes were strewn across the bed in piles that made no organisational sense, half-packed bags yawning open like they weren't quite ready to leave either. I moved slowly, folding the turquoise Thai silk dress Sanjay had made me, smoothing it gently with my palms before placing it in my suitcase. My fingers lingered on the fabric longer than they needed to.

Saying goodbye was folding Sanjay's silk dress into my suitcase, my fingers tracing its seams one last time, as if I could hold onto the warmth of his smile.

I'd met Sanjay in the soft, golden blur of new beginnings. A cocktail bar. A tailored suit. A half-serious joke about a picket fence and Laura Ashley wallpaper. What started as innocent flirting had unravelled into a tenderness I hadn't expected. He'd steadied me when I stumbled through Thai phrases at the market, teased me into laughter when I felt like an outsider, and kissed me under Khaosan's flickering lights, as if the world beyond us had vanished.

We met one final time outside the shop. The neon lights flickered above us, casting strange shadows on the pavement. He was finishing up for the night, folding fabric, locking up like it was any other day.

"So," he said finally. "You're really going?"

I nodded. "Just for now. Home, for a while."

He gave a sad smile. "You always had more places to be."

I stared into his eyes for a moment, but the truth hung unspoken between us. That spark we'd shared belonged to those first golden months—when everything was new and dizzying. We'd found something in each other then—laughing over burnt pad thai in his tiny kitchen, or stealing glances under Khaosan's neon glow, as if we could outshine the chaos. A mirror, maybe. Or a fantasy. But fantasies fade.

"I'm glad I met you," I said, meaning it more than I could say.

He reached out and held my hands, softly, tenderly. "Same, Ellie. You lit things up for a while."

"I got you something," he said, pulling a tiny silver elephant pendant from his pocket. "For luck. And travel. And remembering."

I couldn't speak for a moment. My throat tightened and my heart swelled painfully in my chest. We stood there in silence, everything and nothing left to say. The kiss we shared was softer than all the others, full of things unspoken. There was no drama. No begging. No promises. Just a quiet knowing that this chapter—ours—had reached its natural end.

We didn't cry. It wasn't that kind of goodbye. Just the slow folding of a chapter. A beautiful one, a magical spark that perhaps belonged firmly to those hazy first months in Thailand. With Sanjay, I let myself imagine a different kind of life, one where love and adventure could co-exist. And while things had shifted between us, he would remain a bright spot in my memories—an echo of mango-scented evenings and the feeling of being truly seen.

And now it was time to leave.

I walked one last time through the night markets, past sizzling street food stalls and bootleg DVD stands, the scent of lemongrass and motorbike fumes hanging in the air. Khaosan Road buzzed with the usual cocktail of noise and neon, full of fresh-faced backpackers with Lonely Planet books clutched in their hands and wide eyes full of possibility. I didn't feel like one of them anymore.

I passed the alleyway where Sanjay and I used to dream up that silly little house, glanced toward the cocktail bar where it all began, and kept walking. I wasn't running away—I was moving forward.

Back in my apartment, I finished packing. My suitcase felt like a time capsule: the sarong from Koh Samet, incense from a temple trip, a slightly sun-bleached photo of me and my students making silly faces. The ends of things always felt a little like grief—but this time, it also felt like space.

At the airport, I bought a cheap postcard from a vending machine and scribbled a note to myself:

"Don't forget who you became here."

And though I was heading back to York, I knew I wouldn't stay long. There was still so much of the world to see. Mexico. Europe. China. Who knew?

I wasn't done yet.

Thailand had changed me. It had broken me open and stitched me back together with golden thread. It had shown me beauty in chaos, peace in uncertainty, and strength I didn't know I had.

I tucked the silver elephant pendant into my pocket, its tiny weight a promise of new horizons.

I didn't know where I was going next—Mexico, Europe, China—but I knew I couldn't go back. Thailand had sown the seeds of wanderlust, and my journey had only just begun.

www.ingramcontent.com/pod-product-compliance
Lightning Source LLC
Chambersburg PA
CBHW061224070526
44584CB00029B/3979